25 Science Mini-Books

for Emergent Readers

By Carol Pugliano-Martin

SCHOLASTIC

PROFESSIONAL BOOKS

NEW YORK • TORONTO • LONDON • AUCKLAND • SYDNEY

MEXICO CITY • NEW DELHI • HONG KONG

To Kate Abell, my Bank Street "Science for Teachers" instructor,
who helped me to love science and who let her tarantula
crawl across my foot!

To Deborah, Danielle, and Ingrid for unfailing support
and wonderful ideas!

Cover design by Jaime Lucero
Cover and interior illustrations by Anthony Lewis,
except pages 5–13 by Cary Pillo and page 14 by James Graham Hale
Interior design by Kathy Massaro

ISBN # 0-590-18946-8
Copyright © 1999 by Carol Pugliano-Martin
All rights reserved.
Printed in the U.S.A.

Contents

Introduction

Recently, I met weekly with a first-grader as part of my teacher education program. Ethan loved reading nonfiction books, especially if they were science-related. Of course, I sought to provide him with books that were enjoyable, informative, and on-level for him. This turned out to be harder than I thought. Some books explained scientific concepts, but the language was too advanced. Others touched on science themes, but were a bit fantastic in their presentation. The latter really bothered Ethan. For example, he became quite upset when we read a story I had written about a hermit crab whose friends, after learning that he has outgrown his shell, build him a tiny house, complete with window boxes and shutters. Ethan refused to finish the book with me, citing that hermit crabs live in shells, not houses!

These mini-books are designed for children like Ethan, who are truly interested in science but become overwhelmed by too much text or too many concepts. The books accurately present each topic while maintaining conventions appropriate for early readers, such as rhyme, repetition, predictability, and appealing illustrations that closely match the text. Children will enjoy the process of making their own books that they can color and keep. By cutting and assembling these books themselves, they will hone their fine-motor skills. The visual and hands-on nature of the mini-books enhances learning by tapping into students' various learning styles.

Here are some ways that these books can be used with your students:

- to introduce a science lesson
- to encourage students to read and review at home
- to create a science library for each child in your class
- to celebrate seasonal changes
- to complement your reading instruction program
- to launch creative writing or research projects
- to encourage independent exploration of a particular science topic
- to use as springboards for creative dramatics
- to start a classroom science center

Companion activities that provide ideas for further exploration of each mini-book are included on pages 5–14. These "Curriculum Connections" include hands-on science and art projects, creative writing ideas, and cooperative learning activities to make science lessons interactive and lively. In addition, you'll find suggestions for fun follow-up reading wherever you see a "Bookshelf" note.

I hope that your students will enjoy these science books written especially for them. I also hope that these mini-books will plant the seed for loving science and discovering the joys that it can bring.

— *Carol Pugliano-Martin*

Curriculum Connections

Animals, Animals

Who's in the Egg?

Inside an Egg How do the parts of an egg help an unborn chick grow? Let children take a close-up look inside an unfertilized egg to find out.

1. Have children work in small groups. Provide a raw egg, hand lenses, a bowl, paper towels, pencils, and paper to each group.

2. Copy the diagram and labels below on the chalkboard.

3. Help children crack the eggshell in half and put the egg into a bowl.

4. Have them use a hand lens to examine the shell.

5. Point out the tiny dots on the shell. Explain that these dots have tiny holes in them that help the unborn chick breathe.

6. Help children identify the other parts of the egg. Encourage them to draw a picture of the egg and to label the parts.

Safety Note

Remind children to keep their hands away from their mouths while they work with the egg and to wash their hands after handling it.

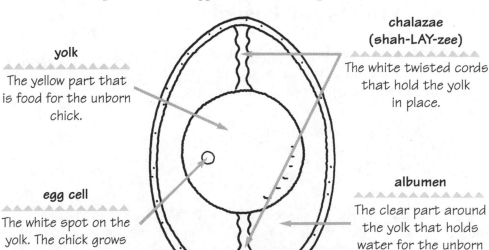

yolk
The yellow part that is food for the unborn chick.

chalazae (shah-LAY-zee)
The white twisted cords that hold the yolk in place.

egg cell
The white spot on the yolk. The chick grows from the egg cell.

albumen
The clear part around the yolk that holds water for the unborn chick.

Bookshelf

Though the text is for older children, the fabulous close-up photos of the monarch's life cycle and migration make **Monarchs** by Kathryn Lasky (Harcourt Brace, 1993) a worthwhile addition to your classroom library.

A Butterfly Grows Up

Butterfly Life Cycle Help children review the stages of a monarch butterfly's life cycle with this art activity. Give each child a piece of construction paper measuring about 5 by 17 inches. Then have them follow these steps.

1. Fold the paper in half, then open it up. Fold each half inward to the center crease, and then refold as necessary so that the pages fold back and forth along the creases like an accordion. Unfold the pages.

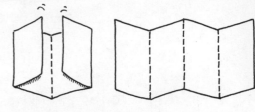

2. On the first page, glue on "milkweed leaves" made from green construction paper. Add a monarch "egg," a single grain of rice.

3. On page 2, glue on a "caterpillar" made from tube- or spiral-shaped pasta that has been painted with yellow, black, and white stripes.

4. On page 3, glue on a "chrysalis" made from shell macaroni that has been painted green and dotted with tiny specks of yellow or gold paint. The chrysalis should hang from the underside of a leaf.

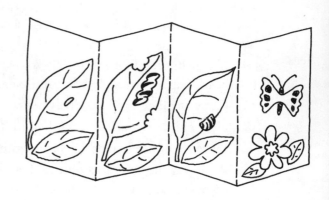

5. On the last page, the monarch emerges! Glue on a piece of bow-shaped pasta. Paint it with black and orange markings.

What Makes an Insect?

Candy Insects To evaluate children's understanding of insect parts, have them make models of insects. Provide candies such as gumdrops, miniature

How to Make the Mini-Books

1. Copy the pages for the books on standard 8 1/2- by 11-inch paper, making single-sided copies.

2. Trim off the shaded edge of each page. Then cut apart the mini-book pages along the solid lines. You should have 8 pages (including the cover) for each book.

3. Put the pages in order with the cover on top. Staple the pages on the left side to make the book.

marshmallows, and shoestring licorice, and toothpicks to attach the parts to each other. Or substitute modeling clay, Styrofoam packing pieces, pipe cleaners, cellophane, tissue paper, and other materials. When the insects are completed, ask: What would a candy spider look like? How would it look different from your insect?

Animals on the Go!

Animal Relay Race Discuss how the different animals in the mini-book move. Then ask children to invent movements that represent each animal. For example, rabbits might hop with bent knees, butterflies might run on tiptoes and flutter their arms, and snakes might wriggle across the floor. Once everyone understands the movements, divide the class into teams and have each team assign a different animal to each teammate. Children then have a relay race in which each animal, in turn, wriggles or flutters or hops across a marked distance. You might also help children time how long each animal takes to travel the distance and then graph the results. Once the race is over, ask: Which animals were the slowest? The fastest? Why?

Shhh! Time to Sleep

Nest Testers Most of the year, chipmunks are active animals. But during winter, when food is scarce, they hibernate—go into an inactive, sleeplike state. Their body temperatures drop and their heart and breathing rates slow down. Help children understand how a chipmunk's nest helps provide insulation from the cold. In a plastic bag, make a "nest" of leaves, grasses, and other plant materials. Let children take turns placing their fist inside the nest in the bag. Then, keeping their fist in the bag, have them place the bag in a pail of cold water. Does the nest keep their fist warm? How is it like a chipmunk's nest? Can children think of ways to make the nest even warmer?

Dinosaurs

Big Book of Dinosaur Records What was the smallest dinosaur? The biggest? Which dinosaur was fastest? Which one ate the most? Make a chart of children's questions about dinosaurs. Then help them research the answers. Invite each child to contribute a page to a class Big Book of Dinosaur Records. Children can record their questions and answers and draw illustrations of their dinosaur.

Bookshelf

Young scientists will enjoy the labeled diagrams that accompany each of the 16 bugs featured in **Bugs** by Nancy Winslow Parker and Joan Richards Wright (Greenwillow, 1987). Lively rhymes complement the informative text.

What Do Animals Do in Winter?: How Animals Survive the Cold by Melvin and Gilda Berger (Chelsea House Publishers, 1998), describes the ways different animals cope with winter's chill, including migration, hibernation, and camouflage.

When It Starts to Snow by Phillis Gershator; illustrated by Martin Matje (Henry Holt, 1998). A boy observes the behaviors of various animals in wintertime and answers the questions, "Where do animals go and what do they do when it snows?" Appealing illustrations and rhyming, patterned text make this a perfect choice for emergent readers.

Animals Around the World

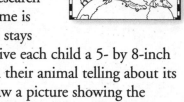

Postcards From Afar Invite children to research one of the animals in the mini-book: what its home is like, how it is adapted to its environment, how it stays safe from danger, what it eats, and so on. Then give each child a 5- by 8-inch index card. Ask children to write a postcard from their animal telling about its life. On the other side of the card, have them draw a picture showing the animal in its habitat. Set up a postcard shop where children can read and "shop" for each other's cards.

Spin, Spider, Spin!

How Does a Web Work? Explain to children how a spider can tell if something has gotten caught in its web. When an insect or other small prey is caught in the web, it struggles to get free. The spider feels the vibrations of the insect's movements along the web and can detect where the insect is in the web. Let children experience this themselves. Divide the class into groups of five. Give each group four long lengths of string. Have children tie each piece around the waist of one group member who is the spider. Have the other group members, the "insects," each take a string and stretch it out. Tell the "spider" to close his or her eyes, and have the insects take turns gently tugging on their strings. Can the spider figure out from which direction the tug is coming?

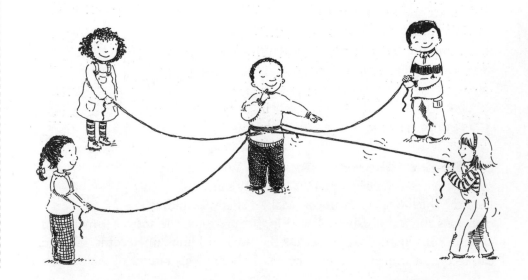

Home Sweet Home

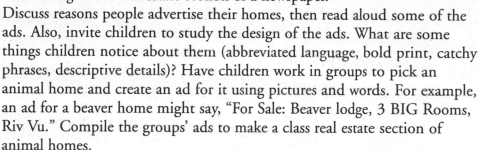

Home for Sale! After reading the mini-book, help children find out more about different animal homes. Then bring in the real estate section of a newspaper. Discuss reasons people advertise their homes, then read aloud some of the ads. Also, invite children to study the design of the ads. What are some things children notice about them (abbreviated language, bold print, catchy phrases, descriptive details)? Have children work in groups to pick an animal home and create an ad for it using pictures and words. For example, an ad for a beaver home might say, "For Sale: Beaver lodge, 3 BIG Rooms, Riv Vu." Compile the groups' ads to make a class real estate section of animal homes.

In the Dark of the Night

Nighttime Animal Mural Invite children to work in small groups to find out more about each of the animals described in the mini-book. They may also like to research other nocturnal animals such as crickets, moths, nightcrawlers, raccoons, and skunks. Then, ask children to draw or paint pictures of their chosen animal and write facts about the animal on sentence strips. Help children display their projects on a bulletin board. Then create nighttime in your classroom by darkening the room. Let group members take turns shining a flashlight on their animal and sharing the facts they learned about it with the rest of the class.

Peek-a-Boo!

Critter Camouflage Help children see firsthand how camouflage helps an animal hide from predators or prey. Take them outdoors and give each child a scrap of cardboard. Tell them that this is their "critter." Ask them to pick a place where their critter will live and to observe the colors and shapes in its habitat. Then challenge them to camouflage their critter with crayons, paint, and other materials. How well can children make their critters blend in with their habitats? Let classmates try to find each other's hidden creatures.

Who Lives in the Pond?

Pond in a Pan Let children create their own miniature ponds. Discuss the animals and plants described in the mini-book. Then pass out aluminum pie pans. Give children clay to create the shoreline, leaving an open space in the middle for the pond. They can create landscapes with twigs, pebbles, and sand; reeds and cattails with colored toothpicks or pieces of straw; ducks, fish, frogs, and other animals with colored Plasticine. Then pour water into the pans, add a few drops of blue food coloring, and stir. Sprinkle green glitter "duckweed" or "algae" over the surface. Then invite children to go on a "field trip" around the classroom to observe their classmates' ponds.

Birds Build Nests

For the Birds! Let children supply materials for birds to use in building their nests. Have children loosely weave materials such as string, yarn, ribbon, straw, bits of fabric, cotton, and hair through the open spaces of a plastic berry box or net bag (like an onion bag). Use a piece of string to hang the box from a tree branch or bush that's in view from your classroom windows, if possible. Let children observe their supply box. What kinds of birds take items from the box? What kinds of materials do they take?

How My Body Works

Growing Up

My Life Timeline Ask children to think about some important things that have happened in their lives. Then invite them to record these events in pictures and words on a timeline as shown. If possible, have them write the year below each event. (Family members may be able to help recall these details.) Children may include events such as when they learned to talk, when they began to walk, when they lost their first tooth, when they started school, when they learned to write their name, and so on.

My Body Is My Buddy

Body Riddle Rhymes Challenge children to tell which part of the body each of the following riddles tells about.

- Snip, rip, grind, crunch, we help you to eat your lunch! What are we? (teeth)
- Like a spread on a bed, I cover your head! What am I? (hair or skin)
- I turn, bend, and twist. On top of me your head sits! What am I? (neck)

Then invite children to make up their own rhyming riddles about different body parts, such as eyes, ears, noses, bones, and muscles. Volunteers can take turns reading the riddles aloud. Can they stump their classmates?

My Five Senses

Senses Team Up This activity reinforces the idea that our five senses often work together. First, have children look through magazines and cut out pictures of people doing different activities. Next, have children create their own chart by writing the five senses down the left side and pasting their pictures along the bottom, as shown. Then invite students to record the senses that the people in each picture are using by checking the appropriate boxes. For example, children might check seeing, smell, and touch for a picture showing a person walking in a flower-filled meadow. Finally, help children interpret the information on the chart. Which senses were used most and least often? Afterward, let children choose a picture and write about what the person in the picture might see, hear, smell, feel, or taste.

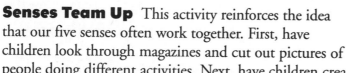

The Senses

hearing			✓		
seeing	✓	✓	✓	✓	✓
taste		✓			✓
smell	✓	✓			✓
touch	✓	✓	✓	✓	✓

Bookshelf

Lively text and whimsical illustrations explain how the five senses work in Joanna Cole's *You Can't Smell a Flower With Your Ear! All About Your 5 Senses* (Putnam/Grosset, 1994). Children will enjoy doing the simple "try this" activities that illustrate, for example, how our sense of smell helps us know how foods taste.

I Am Healthy!

Good Health Pantomimes Invite children to act out the motions described in the mini-book. Then ask them to write and illustrate their own "We Are Healthy!" class big book. First, generate a list of things that they do to stay healthy (such as playing sports or eating nutritious foods). Let children work individually or in teams to create a page for the book. Then bind the pages together with a front and back cover. Invite volunteers to act out the various motions described on each page as the class reads it aloud.

Recipe for a Plant

Recipe for a Plant

Sprout-a-Seed Necklaces Have children make a
necklace that lets them watch seeds sprout. Collect small,
clean, clear plastic pill containers or spice jars. Then give
each child a container, a piece of moistened cotton, several seeds (alfalfa, radish,
or grass seeds work well), and an 18-inch length of yarn or string. Show
children how to put the cotton inside the container, place the seeds between
the cotton and the side of the container, and put the lid on. Then have them
tie the yarn around the lid, knot the ends, and put their necklaces on. As
children watch their seeds for changes, explain that seeds can sprout without
soil as long as they get air and water. (The air in the closed containers will be
sufficient to allow the seeds to sprout.) After they sprout, transfer the seeds to
larger containers with soil so that they can continue to grow.

Sunflower Helpers

Sunflower Helpers

Sunflower Mural Sunflowers can grow as tall as
20 feet, but average around 6 feet tall. Let students
create a life-size sunflower to review the "helpers" that
make these amazing plants grow.

1. Lay a six-foot piece of bulletin board paper on the floor. Make roots by
   gluing down pieces of brown yarn. For soil, spread glue around the
   roots and sprinkle with coffee grounds. Or color around the roots with
   brown crayons.
2. Build the tall stem with empty cardboard rolls from gift wrap, painted
   green. Fit one inside the other, cut to size, and glue down. Attach green
   construction paper leaves (or use crepe paper, which can be shaped to
   create more lifelike leaves).
3. Make bees by painting cotton balls and attaching features snipped from
   construction paper. Glue these onto the sunflower.
4. Attach the mural to the wall. Add a big, bright, construction paper sun.
   Children can add labels describing the job of each sunflower "helper."

Seeds on the Go

Seeds on the Go

Travel Tests Let children test and classify seeds
based on the way they travel. Collect a variety of seeds
(milkweed seeds, dandelion parachutes, cockleburs,
pussy willows, sycamore seeds, maple seeds, and acorns). Also have on hand

Bookshelf

A young girl raises
sunflowers from
seeds in **Backyard
Sunflower** by
Elizabeth King
(Dutton, 1993).
Stunning color
photos make this
book a standout.

a few wool socks or mittens or stuffed animal toys, bowls of water, and straws. Label four paper plates: GRABBER, FLOATER, WIND DRIFTER, and SPINNER. Then model how to do each test and how to sort the seeds on the labeled plates based on the test results.

- **GRABBER TEST** Press a fuzzy sock, mitten, or a stuffed animal on top of the seed. If it sticks, the seed is a "grabber."
- **FLOATER TEST** Place the seed in water. If it floats, the seed goes on the "floater" plate.
- **WIND DRIFTER TEST** Place the seed on a desk and blow on it gently with a straw. If it moves, it's a "wind drifter."
- **SPINNER TEST** Hold the seed above your head and drop it. If the seed spins as it falls, it goes on the "spinner" plate.

An Apple Tree's Year

Apple Tree In-the-Round Books Let children create their own books to record a year in the life of an apple tree. Give each child four small paper plates. Then set up four stations where children can draw, paint, and use craft materials to show how an apple tree looks during each season. Branches painted with watered-down glue and sprinkled with salt produce a snowy effect for winter; crumpled pieces of pink tissue paper make delicate apple blossoms; red cinnamon candies or small beads can be used for apples; and leaves cut out from red, orange, and yellow construction paper work well for autumn. Then punch holes in the plates and use a brass fastener or O-ring to hold the pages together. To see the changes in their apple tree, children fan out the pages.

Fruit or Vegetable? A Guessing Game

Fruit or Vegetable? Fold-Ups Bring in an assortment of the fruits and vegetables described in the mini-book. Hold up different plant products and ask children to decide whether each is a fruit. To check their guesses, cut open the foods to look for seeds. Then let children make fold-up books to record their discoveries. Give each child an 8-inch square of construction paper. Show them how to fold each corner into the center as shown. On each outside flap, have them draw and label a different fruit or vegetable. Inside, on the middle square, children write "Fruit or Vegetable?" Inside each flap, children draw how the plant product looks inside and write whether it is a fruit or a vegetable. Children will enjoy taking home their fold-ups to test their family members' knowledge about fruits and vegetables.

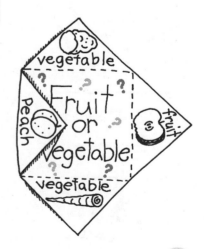

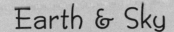

Earth & Sky

Look Up in the Sky

Sky-Watch Banners Help children find out more about the awesome sights that fill the sky. Divide the class into groups and assign each group a different celestial object or sky phenomenon to research. Also encourage children to make their own observations of the moon, clouds, stars, and so on. (Tell children not to look directly at the sun, however.) Then let the class create a sky-watch banner to share what they learned. Place a roll of bulletin board paper on the floor. Let each group take turns drawing, painting, and writing captions about the topic they studied. Provide other materials, such as glitter and glue to help stars twinkle, cotton to make clouds fluffy, and shiny yellow paint to make bright, shiny suns. (To make the paint, mix 1 cup of corn syrup with about 20 drops of food coloring.) Display the banner in the hallway for everyone to enjoy!

All Kinds of Weather

The Weather Channel Invite children to become television weather forecasters! Cut out the bottom of a large cardboard box, like the carton a TV comes in. Then cut out a window in one side, leaving a border of a few inches around the opening. Invite children to help decorate the box to look like a TV. (They might glue on milk jug caps for channel knobs and add an antenna made out of pipe cleaners, for example.) Use sturdy tape to attach the box to a bulletin board so that the "TV screen" faces out. Encourage children to bring in weather reports from the newspaper. If possible, also tape weather reports from television to show to students. Discuss the elements that make a good broadcast. Then let children take turns presenting daily weather reports on your classroom TV.

Clouds

Catch a Cloud Let children make viewfinders to help them catch a cloud! Give each child half of a file folder. Show them how to fold it in half and cut a window out of the center. Then have them unfold it and tape a craft stick near one end. Around the frame, let children draw pictures of the different kinds of clouds they might see. Take children outside on a day when there are lots of clouds in the sky. Tell them to "catch" a cloud inside their frames. Encourage children to name shapes, people, animals, or other things that their clouds resemble. (Caution children to protect their eyes by not looking directly at the sun.)

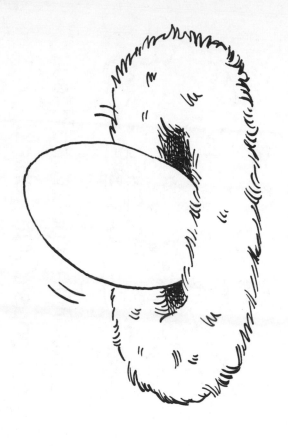

Who's in the Egg?

1

Look! The egg begins to shake.

3

Look! There is a tiny hole.

2

Look! The eggshell starts to break.

7

Look! With a push and a kick,
out pops a fluffy chick!

5

Look! What's this egg going to do?

6

Look! What is that poking through?

4

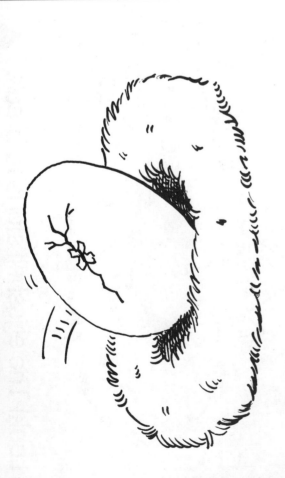

Look! The egg wobbles and rolls.

A Butterfly Grows Up

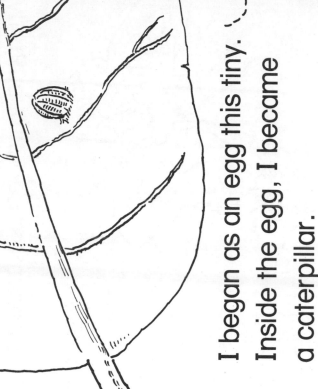

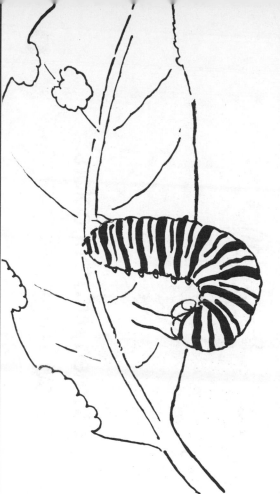

①

I began as an egg this tiny.
Inside the egg, I became
a caterpillar.

③

Then I hung from a leaf and
changed into a chrysalis.

②

After I hatched, I ate a lot
and grew and grew and grew!

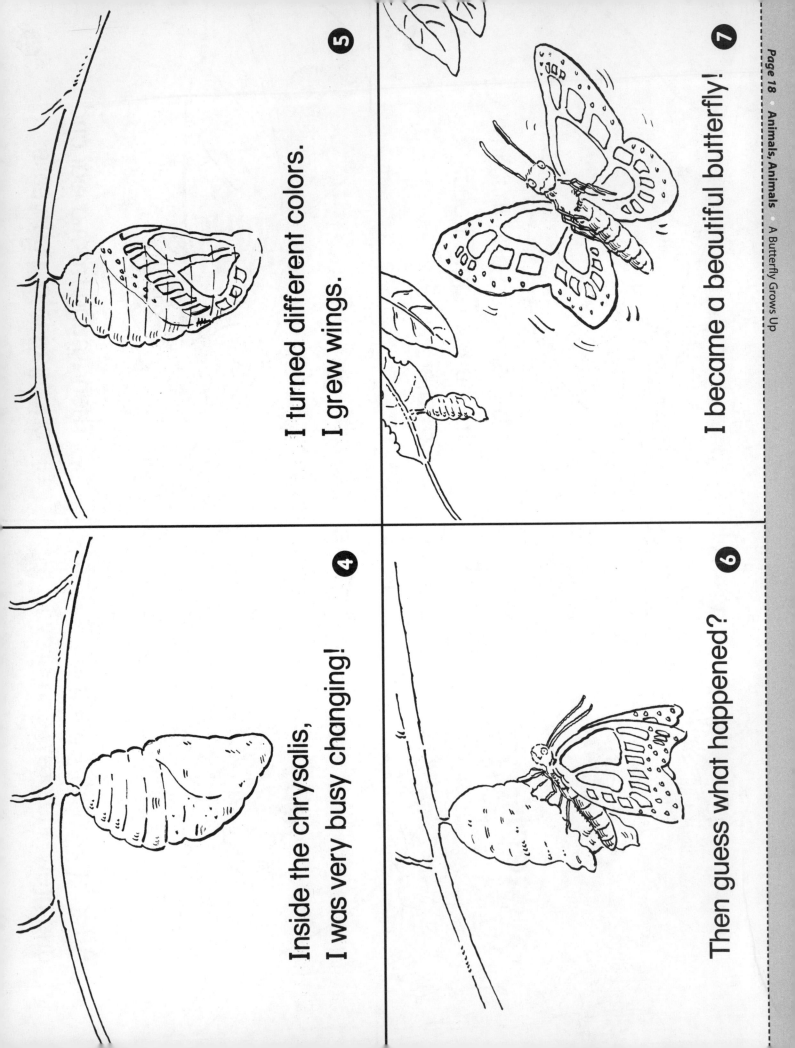

4 Inside the chrysalis, I was very busy changing!

5 I turned different colors. I grew wings.

6 Then guess what happened?

7 I became a beautiful butterfly!

What Makes an Insect?

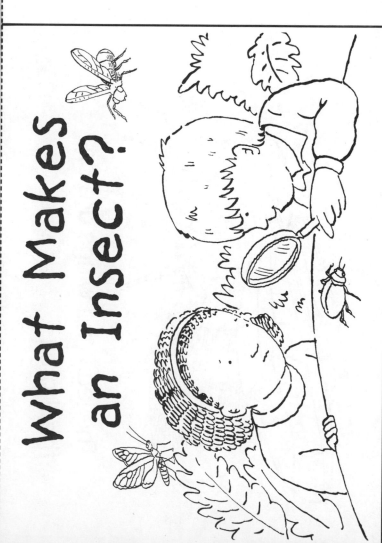

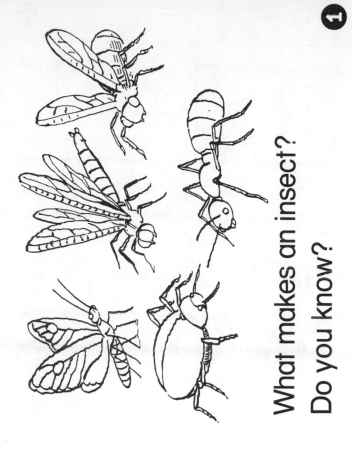

What makes an insect?
Do you know?

1

Insects have six legs,
no more and no less.

2

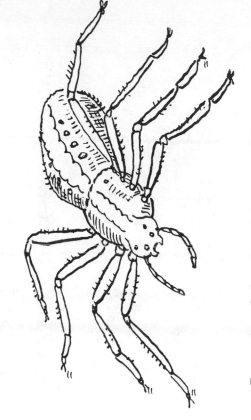

Is a spider an insect?
See if you can guess!

3

5

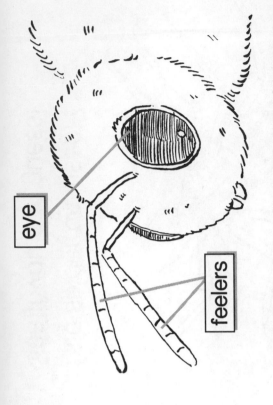

eye

feelers

An insect's feelers and eyes are on its head.

7

What makes an insect? Now you know!

4

head

thorax

abdomen

An insect has three body parts: a head, a thorax, and an abdomen.

6

The legs and wings are on the thorax.

Animals on the Go!

1

Rabbits hop.

2

Snakes slither.

3

Butterflies flap their wings and flitter.

7

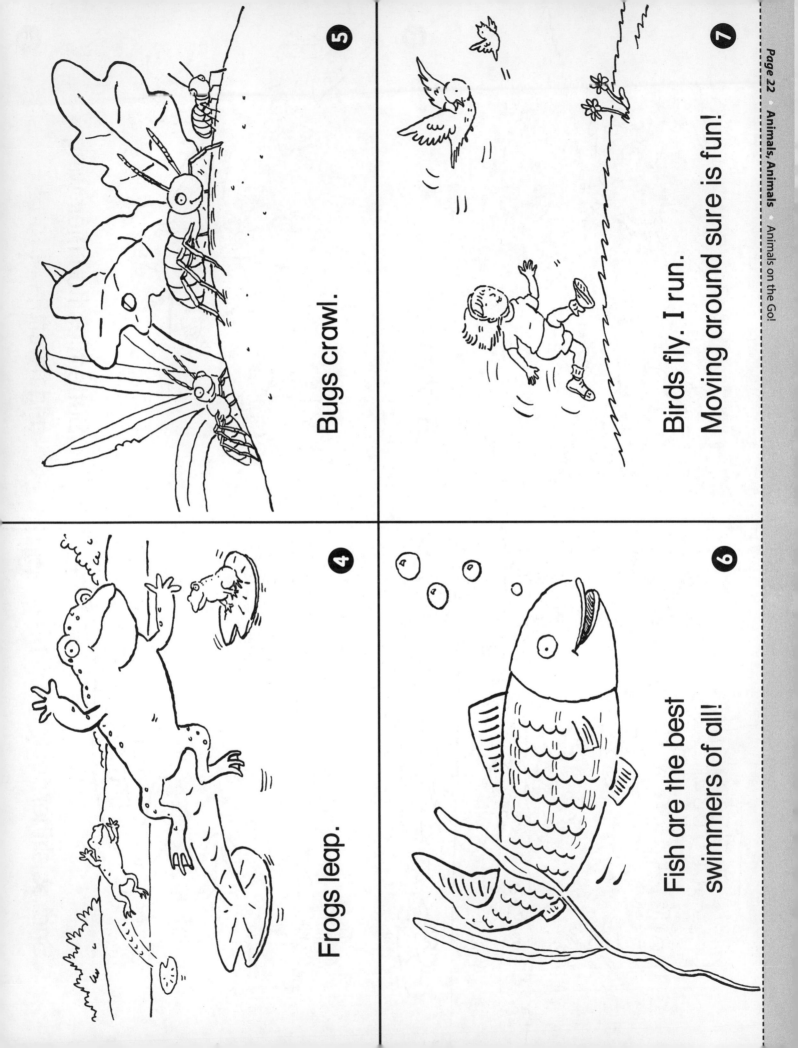

Birds fly. I run.
Moving around sure is fun!

5

Bugs crawl.

6

Fish are the best
swimmers of all!

4

Frogs leap.

Shhh! Time to Sleep

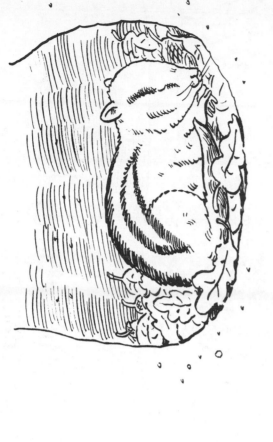

Shhh! The chipmunk is sleeping.

1

It will sleep through the winter.

2

In the fall, the chipmunk gathered lots of food.

3

7

But until then.... Shhh!

5

In the hole, it made a soft bed.

6

The chipmunk will wake up in the spring.

4

It found a hole where it would be safe.

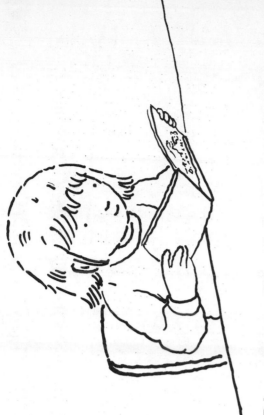

Dinosaurs

Dinosaurs lived a long time ago.
There aren't any left, you know.

1

Some dinosaurs walked on two legs.
Others walked on four.

2

Some dinosaurs were quiet.
Others would roar!

3

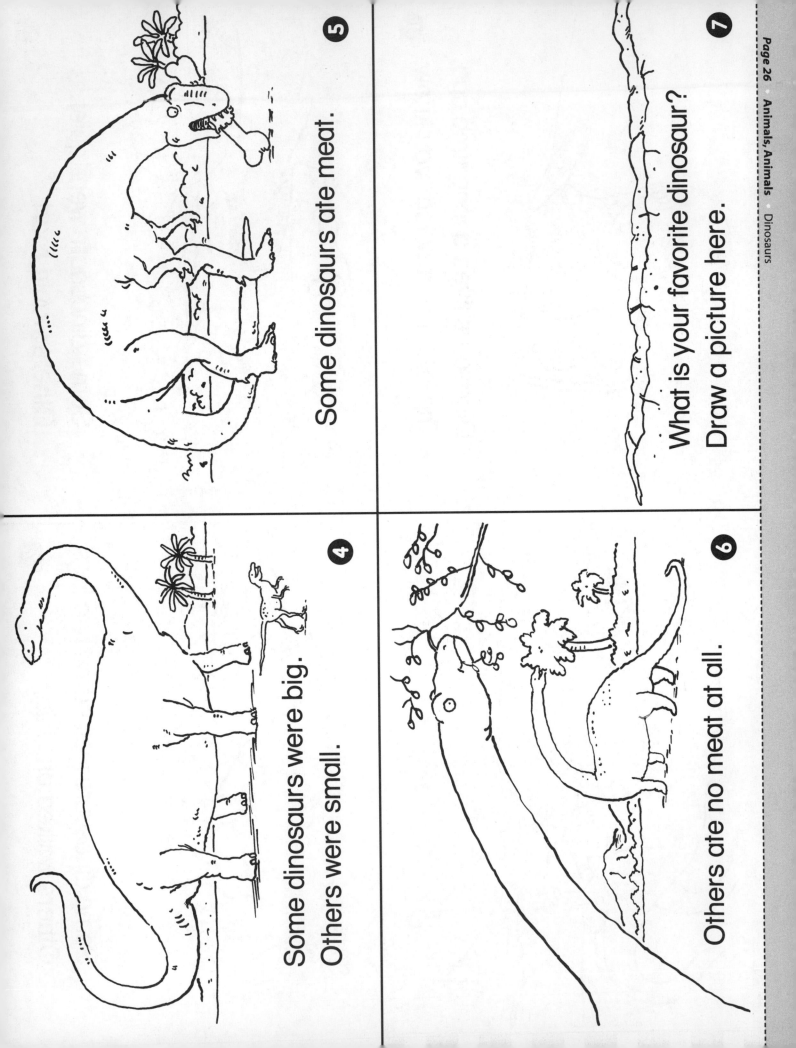

Some dinosaurs ate meat.

5

Some dinosaurs were big.
Others were small.

4

What is your favorite dinosaur?
Draw a picture here.

7

Others ate no meat at all.

6

Animals Around the World

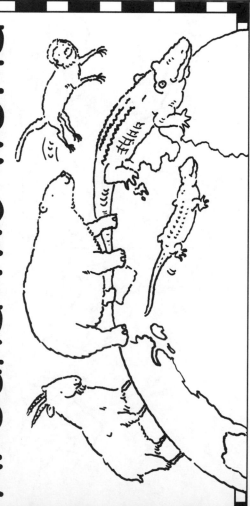

1

A lizard roams over the desert sand.

3

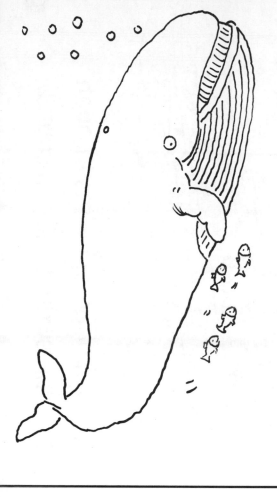

A whale swims in the deep blue sea.

2

A polar bear moves across the frozen Arctic land.

5

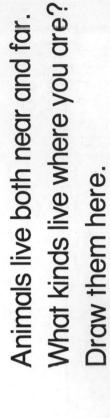

An alligator swims through the swamp with no sound.

7

Animals live both near and far.
What kinds live where you are?
Draw them here.

4

A monkey swings from a rain forest tree.

6

A mountain goat climbs up rocks to get around.

1

Bit by bit,

2

bit by bit,

3

the spider spins its web.

Spin, Spider, Spin!

7

Now it's a beautiful web where the spider can stay all day long!

5

bit by bit,

6

the strands get nice and strong.

4

Bit by bit,

What is home for a bear?

1

What is home for a beaver?

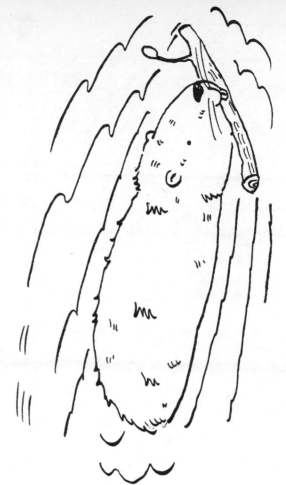

3

A cave is home for a bear.

2

⑤

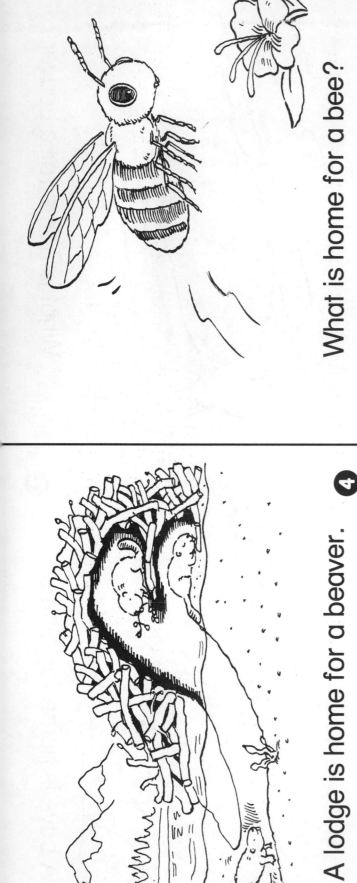

What is home for a bee?

⑦

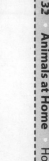

And my home is a home for me!

④

A lodge is home for a beaver.

⑥

A hive is home for a bee.

In the Dark of the Night

1

Bats prowl,
in the dark of the night.

2

Coyotes howl,
in the dark of the night.

3

Frogs splash,
in the dark of the night.

5

Owls hoot,
in the dark of the night.

7

While you sleep tight, a lot goes on
in the dark of the night!

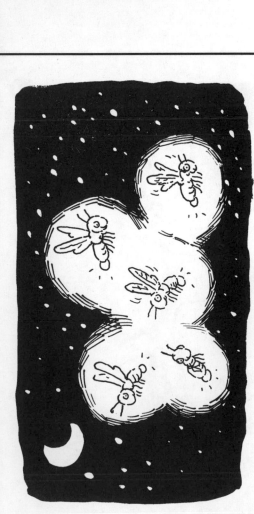

4

Lightning bugs flash,
in the dark of the night.

6

Mice scoot,
in the dark of the night.

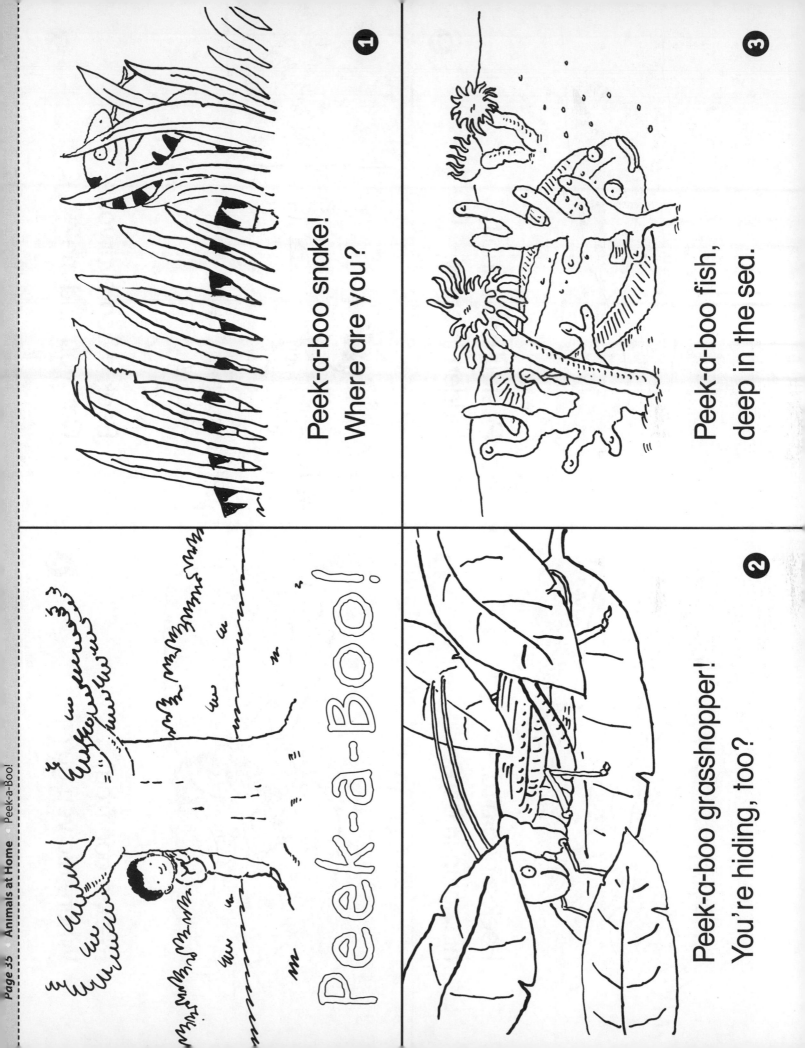

①

Peek-a-boo snake!
Where are you?

③

Peek-a-boo fish,
deep in the sea.

Peek-a-Boo!

②

Peek-a-boo grasshopper!
You're hiding, too?

7

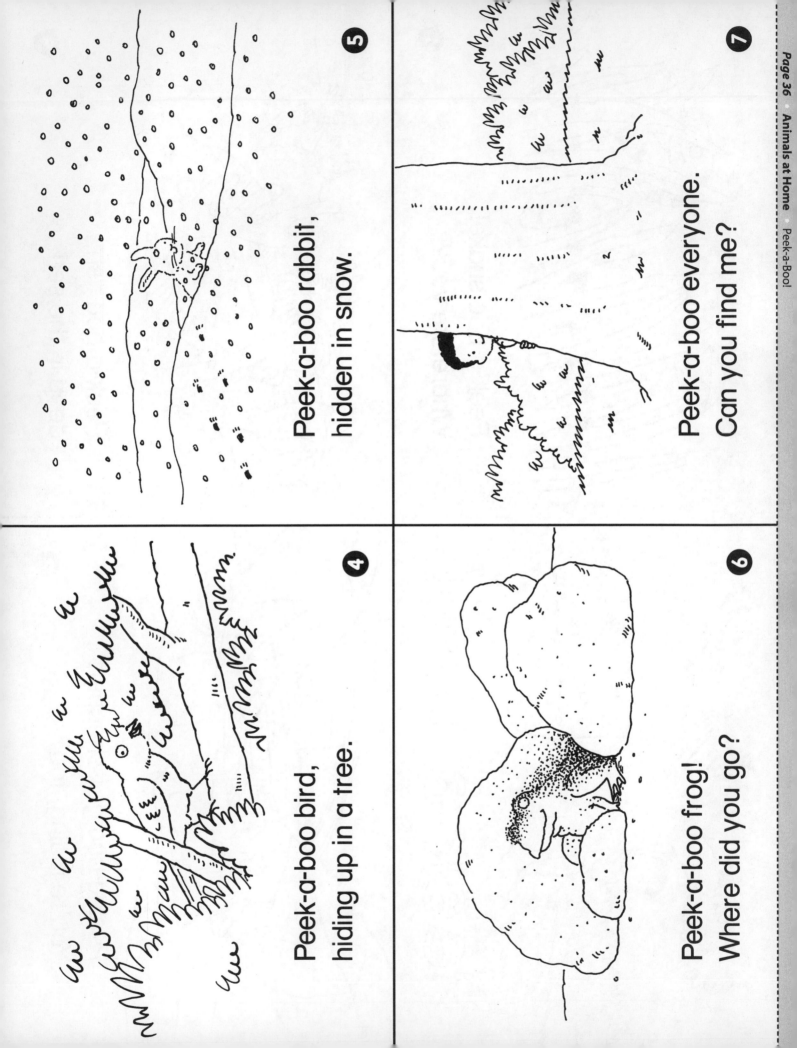

Peek-a-boo everyone.
Can you find me?

5

Peek-a-boo rabbit,
hidden in snow.

6

Peek-a-boo frog!
Where did you go?

4

Peek-a-boo bird,
hiding up in a tree.

Who Lives in the Pond?

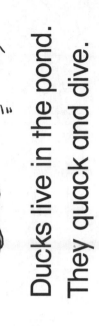

❶

Ducks live in the pond.
They quack and dive.

❸

Fish live in the pond.
They dart and swim.

❷

Plants live in the pond.
They grow and sway.

5

Salamanders live in the pond.
They scurry and hide.

7

They all live in the pond together.
That's what they do!

4

Frogs live in the pond.
They hop and croak.

6

Beavers live in the pond.
They build and chew.

Birds Build Nests

1

Some birds make their nests from sticks.

2

Others use hair.

3

Some birds make their nests from mud.

7

No matter how they are made, each nest is a home.

5

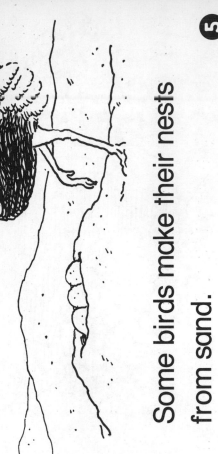

Some birds make their nests from sand.

6

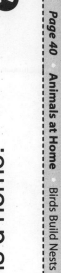

Others use stones.

4

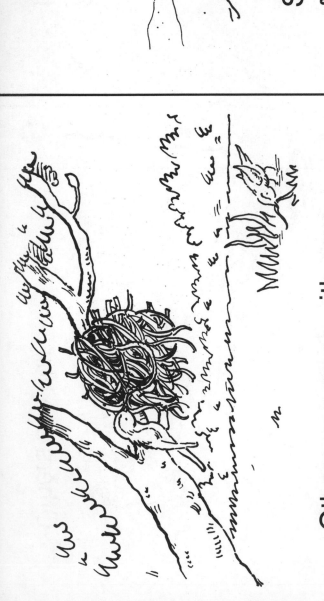

Others use grass with care.

Growing Up

1

The lamb was born,

2

just like me.

3

The lamb learned to talk,

5

The lamb learned to walk,

4

just like me.

7

And the lamb is loved, just like me!

6

just like me.

My Body Is My Buddy

1

My body is my buddy.
It helps me every day.

2

My muscles help me move
so that I can play.

3

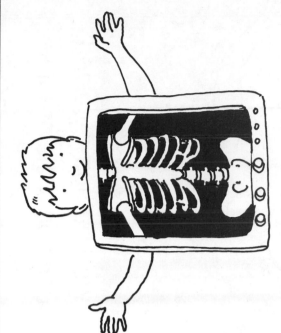

My bones help me stand up
so very straight and tall.

7

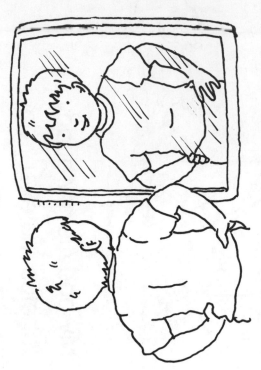

I'm glad I have a buddy like my body!

6

My brain helps me think about everything I read!

5

My heart pumps my blood.
My lungs help me breathe.

4

My skin protects my bones and muscles like a strong wall.

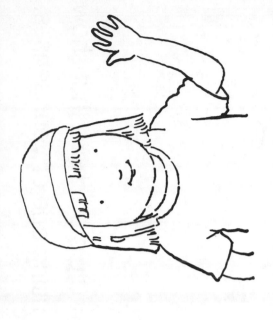

❶

I have five senses.
They are helpful as can be.

❸

My hands help me touch.

Hearing

Smell

Taste

Touch

Seeing

My Five Senses

❷

My nose helps me smell.
My eyes help me see.

7

Draw a picture here that shows you using one of your senses.

5

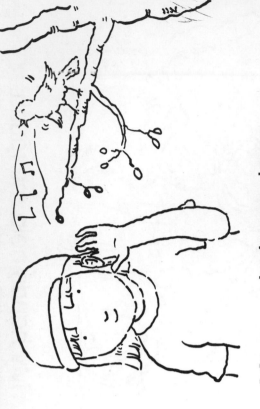

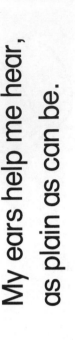

My ears help me hear, as plain as can be.

6

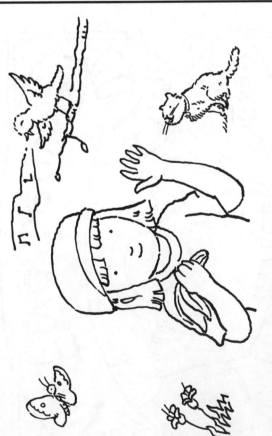

Yes, I have five senses. And five is fine with me!

4

My tongue helps me taste. Not a sense goes to waste!

1

I am healthy.
Scrub! Scrub! Scrub!

3

I am healthy.
Crunch! Crunch! Crunch!

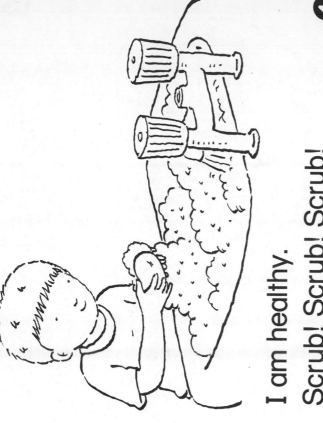

I Am Healthy!

2

I am healthy.
Brush! Brush! Brush!

7

I am healthy.
Hooray! Hooray! Hooray!

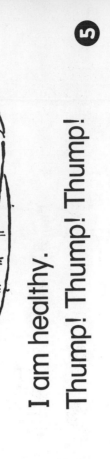

5

I am healthy.
Thump! Thump! Thump!

6

I am healthy.
Look! Look! Look!

4

I am healthy.
Jump! Jump! Jump!

Recipe for a Plant

How do you grow a plant?
It's easy!

1

Take some dirt.

2

Add a seed.

3

⑤

Wait a while.

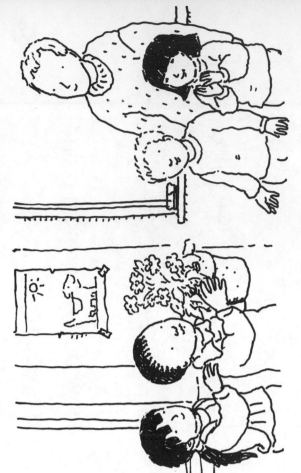

⑦

Share your plant with everyone!

④

Pour some water,
only as much as you need.

⑥

Add lots of sun.

Sunflower Helpers

1

A beautiful sunflower stands in the sun.

It has many helpers.
Let's meet every one.

flower

leaves

roots

seeds

stem

2

3

The roots bring water from the soil to the stem.

4

The stem brings water to the leaves, like a straw.

5

The leaves gather sunlight to help the plant grow.

6

Bees bring pollen from one sunflower to another.

7

Pollen helps make seeds so new sunflowers can grow!

water

Seeds on the Go

Seeds are always on the go.

1

A squirrel hides seeds
for a winter treat.

3

A bird drops a seed from its beak.

2

7

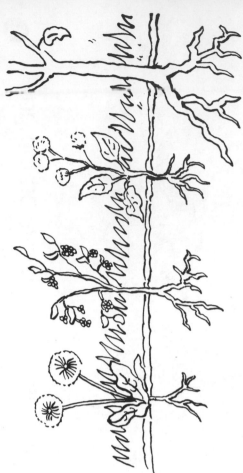

Plants need room to grow big and tall. Now there is room for them all!

5

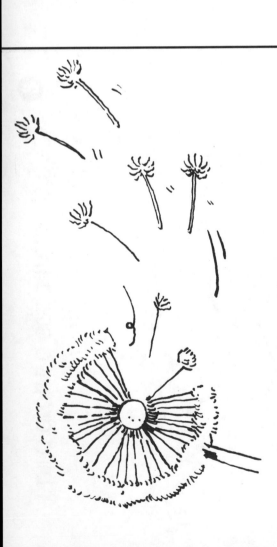

Even feet bring seeds from here to there!

6

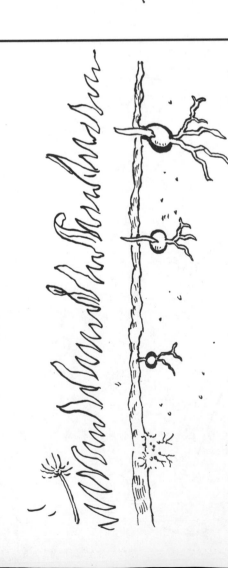

Seeds are always on the go, finding new places to grow.

4

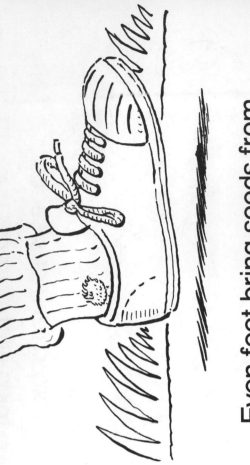

The wind blows seeds through the air.

An Apple Tree's Year

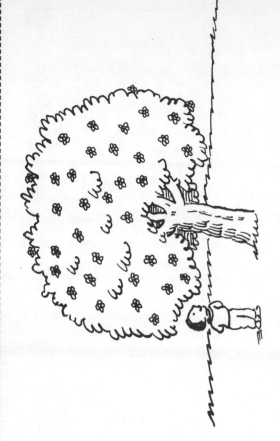

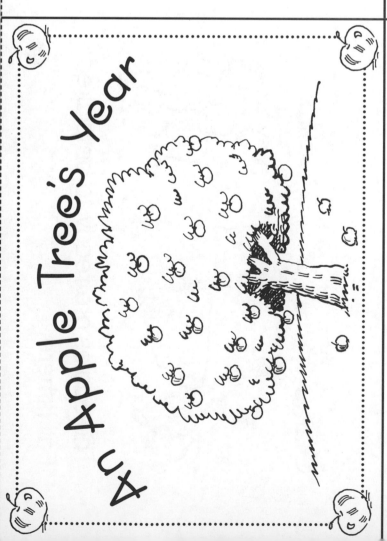

1

An apple tree tells you what season it is. Just take a look!

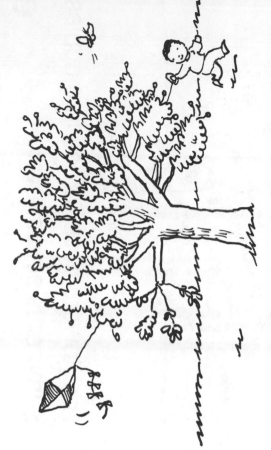

3

The apple tree's leaves and tiny buds tell you that it is spring.

2

The apple tree's bare branches tell you that it is winter.

7

How can you enjoy the apples?
Write your idea here.

5

The flowers have turned into apples!
Summer is almost over.

6

The apples are ready to be picked!
Fall is here.

4

The apple tree's pretty flowers
tell you that summer is near!

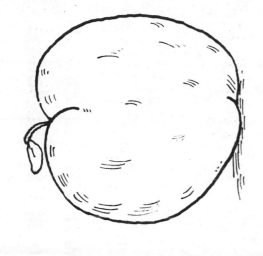

Fruit or Vegetable?

A Guessing Game

①

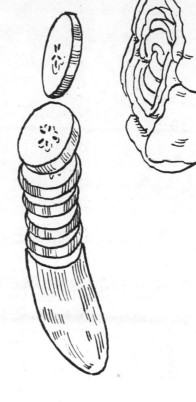

Any food with seeds is a fruit.
Is a peach a fruit?

③

Yes, a cucumber is a fruit!

Is lettuce a fruit?

②

Yes, a peach is a fruit.

Is a cucumber a fruit?

7

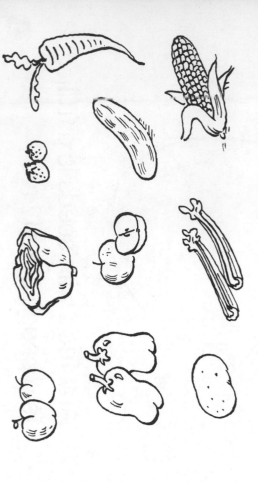

Draw a circle around all the fruits in this picture.

5

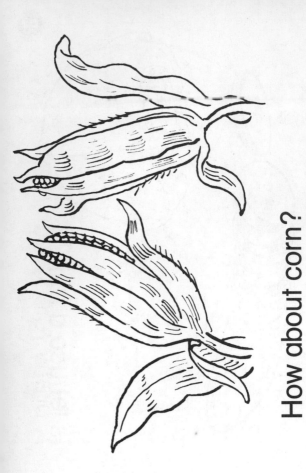

How about corn?
Is corn a fruit or a vegetable?

6

Corn is a fruit.
Its kernels are seeds.

4

No, lettuce is a vegetable.
It has no seeds.

Look Up in the Sky

Look up in the sky. What do you see?
In daytime, the sun shines on me. ❶

Fluffy white clouds float on by. ❷

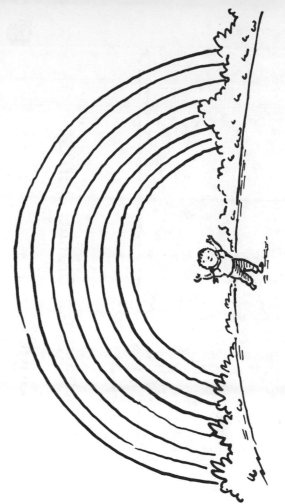

A pretty rainbow colors the sky. ❸

⑤

And stars look like gems
so bright.

⑦

Make a wish!
But don't tell, so it will come true!

④

At night, the moon gives lots
of light.

⑥

Sometimes a shooting star will
pass on through.

1

Wind blows my hat.

All Kinds of Weather

3

Lightning is bright.

2

Thunder is loud.

7

What is your favorite kind of weather?
Draw it here.

5

The sun warms the earth
and helps plants grow.

6

And often in winter,
there is frosty white snow!

4

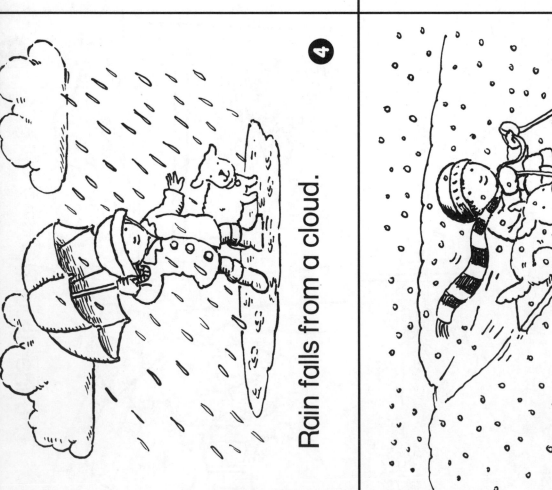

Rain falls from a cloud.

Clouds

1 Some clouds look like horses.

2 Some clouds look like cars.

3 Some clouds look like houses.

7 Sometimes when it's sunny, there are no clouds at all!

6 They make the rain fall.

5 Some clouds are dark gray.

4 Some clouds look like stars.